Andrew Samuel Fuller

The Illustrated Strawberry Culturist

Andrew Samuel Fuller

The Illustrated Strawberry Culturist

ISBN/EAN: 9783744678445

Printed in Europe, USA, Canada, Australia, Japan

Cover: Foto ©ninafisch / pixelio.de

More available books at **www.hansebooks.com**

THE
ILLUSTRATED
STRAWBERRY CULTURIST:

CONTAINING THE

HISTORY, SEXUALITY, FIELD AND GARDEN CULTURE OF STRAW-
BERRIES, FORCING OR POT CULTURE, HOW TO
GROW FROM SEED, HYBRIDIZING,

AND ALL OTHER INFORMATION NECESSARY TO ENABLE EVERYBODY TO RAISE
THEIR OWN STRAWBERRIES; TOGETHER WITH A DESCRIPTION OF NEW
VARIETIES AND A LIST OF THE BEST OF THE OLD SORTS.

FULLY ILLUSTRATED.

By ANDREW S. FULLER

*Author of the " Grape Culturist," " Small Fruit Culturist," " Practical
Forestry," Etc., Etc.*

NEW YORK:
ORANGE JUDD COMPANY,
52 AND 54 LAFAYETTE PLACE,
1911

PRINTED IN U. S. A.

PREFACE.

It is now twenty-five years since I wrote the first edition of the STRAWBERRY CULTURIST. At that time but little attention had been paid to the cultivation of this best of all berries, and, with the exception of an occasional basket or crate of the Hovey and Wilson, New York markets were mostly supplied with the little Crimson Cone and Scotch Runner raised in New Jersey.

From time to time new varieties had been introduced at home and from abroad, and by copying all the names found in both European and American nurserymen's catalogues, I was enabled to make a list of nearly five hundred varieties, of which only a few survive. Among these may be named the Hovey, Wilson, Triomphe de Gand, Lennig's White, Downer's Prolific and the Monthly Alpines, but, with one or two exceptions, these are very sparingly cultivated. The others have been discarded for inferiority of size or flavor, lack of productiveness, want of adaptability to a wide range of climate and soils, or for other good and sufficient reasons, and their places have been filled by varieties supposed to be better, and in such numbers as to confuse seekers after the best. But which is or are the best of all the varieties known would be a difficult question to answer; for the one that gives entire satisfaction in one section often proves a failure in another, and only experiments or close observation will teach one how to choose. Much credit is certainly due to those who have aided in producing new varieties, but the perfect Strawberry, equally well adapted to all kinds of soils and climates has not as yet appeared in cultivation.

During the last quarter of a century botanists have somewhat changed their ideas in regard to the number and distribution of the species of the Strawberry, and while this may be of no especial importance to the practical cultivator of this fruit, still I have arranged the species to conform to the more recent discoveries of our botanists.

As regards the culture of the Strawberry I find little to change and less to add. In writing the STRAWBERRY CULTURIST (my first attempt at book making) I aimed to give the public the result of my practical experience in plain words. I have since that time experimented largely, but have learned nothing that induces me to change materially the directions therein given.

This little treatise has been re-written to supply a want of the present generation, and, with the hope that it will serve as did its predecessor to stimulate its readers in renewed efforts to produce the best of Berries and in the greatest abundance, I send it forth on its humble mission.

ANDREW S. FULLER.

RIDGEWOOD, N. J., Jan., 1887.

THE STRAWBERRY CULTURIST.

THE STRAWBERRY.

A genus of low perennial stemless herbs with runners, and leaves divided into three leaflets ; calyx open and flat ; petals five, white ; stamens ten to twenty, sometimes more ; pistils numerous, crowded upon a cone-like head in the center of the flower. Seeds naked on the surface of an enlarged pulpy receptacle called the fruit.

The Strawberry belongs to the great Rose family, and the name of the genus is *Fragaria*, from the Latin *Fraga*, its ancient name. The French name of the strawberry is *Fraisier ;* German, *Erdbeerpflanze ;* Italian, *Planta di fragola ;* Dutch, *Aadbezie ;* Spanish, *Freza.* The South American Spaniards call the wild Strawberries of the country, *Frutila.*

The well-known unstable character of the species makes it rather difficult to determine the limit of variation, but the following classification is in accord with the experience of practical cultivators of the Strawberry as well as with the more recent arrangement of the species in botanical works.

Fragaria vesca.—The common wild Strawberry of Europe, including both the White and Red Wood, also the annual and Monthly Alpine Strawberries. Of the latter there are varieties with both white and red fruit,

5

growing in stools or clumps producing no **runners**, or **very** sparingly. This species is also indigenous to **North America** and found plentifully in our more northern States, and westward to the Rocky Mountains, where it grows in the more elevated and cooler regions. The plants are slender, with thin, often pale-green leaflets; fruit small, oval, oblong, or sharp pointed; seeds quite prominent, never depressed.

Fragaria Californica.—A low-growing species closely allied to the *F. vesca*, but thought to be specifically distinct by some botanists. The entire plant covered with spreading hairs; leaves rather thin, wedge-shape and broadest at the tip. Flowers, small white; calyx shorter than the petals, and often toothed or cleft; fruit small, and seed as in *vesca*. On the hills and mountains of California and in northern **Mexico**. There are no varieties of this species in cultivation.

Fragaria Virginiana.—The Wild Strawberry of the United States east of the Rocky Mountains. Plant, with few or numerous scattering hairs; upper surface of leaves often very dark green and shining, also very large, thick, coarsely toothed. Flowers, white, in clusters on erect scapes. Fruit red or scarlet, often with long neck; seeds in shallow or deep pits on the surface of the receptacle. This species is the parent of an immense · number of varieties, like the Wilson, Boston Pine, Early Scarlet, &c.

Variety.—**Illinoensis** is found in the rich soils of the Western States and is a larger and coarser growing plant, more villous or hairy than the species, and the fruit is usually of a lighter color. Some of the most popular varieties in cultivation are descended from this indigenous western variety, such as the Charles Downing, **Downer's Prolific**, &c.

Fragaria Chiliensis.—A widely distributed species, especially on the west coast of America, where it is found from Alaska on the north, southward to California, and thence to Chili and other countries in South America. It is usually a low-growing, spreading plant with large thick cuneate, obovate leaflets, smooth and shining above ; with silky appressed hairs underneath. Fruit stalks very stout ; flowers white, large, often more than an inch in diameter and with five to seven petals. Formerly these large flowered varieties from South America were supposed to belong to a distinct species—the *F. grandiflora*, or Great-Flowering Strawberry ; but more recent investigation has shown that all belong to the one species, viz., *F. Chiliensis*. This species is the parent of the most noted European varieties, some of which have long been cultivated in this country, but the varieties of the Virginian and Chili Strawberry have become so intermingled by crossing that it is now scarcely possible to trace their parentage.

Fragaria Indica.—A small species from Upper India, with yellow flowers, and small red, rather tasteless fruit. Often cultivated as a curiosity and ornament, as the plants bear continuously through the summer and autumn.

Fragaria elatior.—Hautbois or Highwood Strawberry. Indigenous to Europe, principally in Germany. Plants tall growing ; fruit usually elevated above the leaves, and the calyx strongly reflexed ; petals small, white ; fruit brownish, pale red, sometimes greenish, with a strong musky, and, to most persons, a disagreeable flavor. Only sparingly cultivated. The plants are inclined to be diœcious, *i. e.*, the two sexes on different plants, even in their wild state.

HISTORY OF THE STRAWBERRY.

How the name of Strawberry came to be applied to
this fruit is unknown, as the old authors do not agree;
some asserting that it was given it because children used
to string them upon straws to sell, while others say that
it took its name from the fact of straw being placed
around the plants in order to keep the fruit clean.   Its
name may not have been derived from either of these,
but from the appearance of the plant ; for when the
ground is covered with its runners, they certainly have
much of the appearance of straw being spread over the
ground.   We have found nothing conclusive on this
point.

The Strawberry does not appear to have been cultivated by the ancients, or even by the Romans, for it is
scarcely mentioned by any of their writers, and then not
in connection with the cultivated fruits or vegetables.
Virgil mentions it only when warning the shepherds
against the concealed adder when seeking flowers and
Strawberries.

> " Ye boys that gather flowers and strawberries,
>   Lo, hid within the grass a serpent lies."

Several other ancient authors mention the Strawberry,
but all refer to it as a wild fruit, not cultivated in gardens ; but there do not appear to have been any improved varieties in cultivation until within about one
hundred years, although the wild plants were transferred
to gardens only in the fifteenth century, as we learn
from works published at that time.

Casper Bauhin, in his " Pinax," published in 1623,
mentions but five varieties.   Gerarde, in 1597, enumer-
ates but three—the white, red, and green fruited.

Parkinson, in 1656, describes the Virginian and
Bohemian, besides those mentioned by Gerarde.   Quin-

tinie, in his "French Gardener," translated by Evelyn in 1672, mentions four varieties, and gives similar directions for cultivation as practised at the present time, viz., planting in August, removing all the runners as they appear, and renewing the beds every four years.

Only four or five varieties are mentioned by any of the writers on gardening earlier than about 150 years ago.

The Fressant Strawberry, mentioned by Quintinie, was the first seedling we find mentioned, and it was claimed to be superior to its parent, the wild Wood or Alpine Strawberry of Europe.

The Hautbois was long supposed to be indigenous to America, and both Parkinson and Miller state that it came from this country, and the former, in his " Paradisus Terrestris," 1629, says that the Hautbois had been with them only of late days, having been brought over from America. It is now known, however, that this species is a native of Germany, where it is called the " Haarbeer."

The Chili Strawberry was formerly supposed to have been introduced into South America by the Spaniards from Mexico; and while plants may have been introduced as stated, still, botanists assure us that the same species is indigenous to both countries. This species was introduced into France by a traveler named Frazier, in 1716, but whether by seeds or living plants is not known. Philip Miller introduced the Chili Strawberry into England in 1729, but he says it was so unproductive that he finally discarded it. He also refers to the irregular shape of the fruit, a characteristic of many of the varieties of this species in cultivation at this time. The varieties of the Chili Strawberry are usually larger and milder in flavor than those of the Virginia

Strawberry, but the plants are rarely as hardy or succeed as well in our Northern States, except in sheltered situations. In Europe, however, the varieties of the Chilian Strawberry have long been preferred to those of the Virginian, probably on account of their large size and mild flavor, as most of our American varieties require a high temperature to develop their saccharine properties.

No improvement was made in the Strawberry by European gardeners until the introduction of the American species, but it was not until the beginning of the present century that practical experiments were made in England for improving this fruit. In 1810 Mr. N. Davidson raised a new variety, which was named the Roseberry. T. A. Knight raised the Downton in 1816; Atkinson, the Grove End Scarlet in 1820; and in 1824 Keen's Seedling appeared. Knight raised the Elton in 1820. During the twenty years from 1810 down to 1830 not more than a half dozen improved varieties were produced in England, but Myatt soon followed with his British Queen, which remained the leading variety of that country for almost a half century.

The French, German, Belgian, and other continental gardeners soon entered the field, and now the Strawberry has become one of the most popular fruits throughout Europe as well as in America.

Although we possessed the materials from which we could have readily produced new and improved varieties of the Strawberry, adapted to our soil and climate, very little was attempted in this direction until long after the Strawberry had become popular in Europe, and even when it began to attract attention in this country, our fruit growers were content to import varieties from abroad instead of attempting to raise new and more valuable ones at home.

The introduction of the Hovey in 1834 proved that it was possible to raise large and productive varieties of the indigenous species, and while a few cultivators may be said to have taken the hint, or avail themselves of this discovery, the larger majority continued to import varieties of the Chili Strawberry only to be sadly disappointed with the result, for, with few exceptions, these are of little value for cultivating in this country.

SEXUALITY OF THE STRAWBERRY.

As the Strawberry belongs to the Rose Family, its flowers should in their natural state contain both stamens and pistils, and they usually do, and the flowers are said to be perfect or bi-sexual. But when plants are taken from their native habitats and placed under cultivation, they often assume forms quite different from their natural ones. Sometimes a particular organ is suppressed, while others are enlarged, and thus we produce deformities and monstrosities among almost every family of cultivated plants.

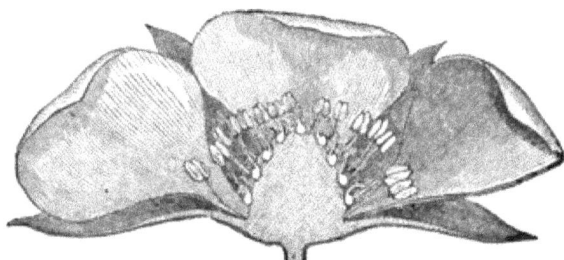

Fig. 1.—CROSS SECTION.

The effects of stimulation or starvation, exposure and protection are different upon different species of plants. The effect of stimulation, through cultivation, upon the Rose proper appears to have forced the stamens to enlarge and become petals circling inward, and smothering the pistils, which are attached to the inside of the rose-like receptacle. But in the Strawberry the receptacle is the reverse of that of the rose, being conical as shown in an enlarged cross-section of a flower, Fig. 1.

Every so-called seed of the Strawberry has one style attached to it; consequently, it is a very important organ, inasmuch as it is through this organ that the influence of the pollen reaches the ovule or seed vessel. The stamens are situated on the calyx, and they may be artifically removed or suppressed by nature, in which case we would have what is called a pistillate flower, which will produce fruit, if the pistils are fertilized from another flower.

Fig. 2.—PISTIL-LATE FLOWER. USUAL SIZE.

It is not important whether a flower produces its own pollen or is supplied from some other source.

Fig. 3.—PISTILLATE FLOWER, ENLARGED.

From some unknown cause the *F. Virginiana* and the *F. elatior* or Hautbois Strawberry of Europe occasionally give varieties in which the stamens or male organs are undeveloped or entirely wanting, and these unisexual plants have long been known as pistillates; the Hovey Strawberry being one of the first to attract special attention in this country. Fig. 2 represents pistillate flower of the usual size, and in Fig. 3

Fig. 4.—PERFECT FLOWER.

the same enlarged. By comparing these with Fig. 4, a perfect flower, and the same enlarged in Fig. 5, the difference may readily be seen.

Fig. 5.—PERFECT FLOWER, ENLARGED.

These abnormal or pistillate varieties are likely to oc-
cur among the seedlings of any of the improved or cultivated varieties, and they are occasionally preserved and
multiplied, although in no instance that has come under
my observation have they proved to be superior to other
varieties with perfect flowers. That they are often preserved and propagated must be considered more as a
matter of personal pride or opinion on the part of the
originator, than a necessity or advantage to fruit growers
in general. But so long as such imperfect varieties are
disseminated, they must be recognized, if for no other
purpose than to place the inexperienced propagator on
his guard against planting them alone, expecting to obtain a crop of fruit. At one time it was supposed or
claimed that these pistillate varieties were, and would
ever remain, totally barren unless fertilized by pollen
from some perfect flowered sort, but as the stamens in
the pistillate varieties are merely suppressed organs, it is
not at all rare to find an occasional one fully developed
and producing pollen. Where this occurs, and it is
frequent in such varieties as the Manchester, a moderate crop of fruit will be produced where no pollen can
reach the flowers from any other source. But these
partly undeveloped stamens cannot be depended upon
for supplying the necessary amount of pollen, and where
varieties designated as pistillates are cultivated, a perfect
flowered one should be grown near by, or even the plants
intermingled in the same bed or row. In cultivating a
pistillate variety a person must set out a perfect flowered one near by, in order to obtain a crop of fruit from
the imperfect ; or, in other words, he must plant two
varieties to be certain of obtaining fruit from the one.
There might be some excuse for this doubling up if the
pistillates were in any way superior to the best of the bi-

sexual or perfect flowered varieties, but as they are not, I fail to see the economy or advantage of cultivating pistillates at all.

When writing the first edition of this work, a quarter of a century ago, I had occasion to refer to the assertion of certain cultivators, who claimed that the pistillate varieties when properly fertilized were more productive than those bearing perfect or bisexual flowers, but facts to substantiate the claim were then wanting, and they certainly have not appeared since, and it is very doubtful if any one cultivating the Strawberry extensively would knowingly select a pistillate in preference to a bisexual variety, provided both were otherwise of equal value.

The best pistillate varieties in cultivation may be fully equal in every respect to the best bisexual or staminates, as they are often termed, but what I claim is that they are no better, besides being objectionable because they must be fertilized by pollen from some other source than their own flowers in order to bear a crop of fruit. This defect in the flowers of the pistillate varieties makes them worthless for cultivating alone in field or garden, for, in order to secure a crop of fruit, a pollen-bearing variety must be cultivated near by, and there is always more or less danger of the plants intermingling, and it can only be prevented by care and attention, while the runners are growing rapidly in summer. There is, however, no real danger of the plants of different varieties intermingling, if they are placed in adjoining beds or rows, and the paths between kept free from runners; but cultivators of the strawberry are often negligent in such matters and mixing of varieties is the result.

INFLUENCE OF POLLEN.

If the small central organs or pistils of a Strawberry flower are not fertilized by pollen from its own stamens or that from some other plant, they soon die away and no fleshy receptacle or fruit is produced. This pollen is an impalpable dust-like powder and yet so important that the production of the Strawberry is dependent upon its presence and potency. There must be not only an abundance of pollen, but it must be supplied by some closely allied species or variety of the Strawberry, to be available. Pollen from the wild or uncultivated Alpines or the Hautbois Strawberries will not fertilize the pistils of the varieties of either the Virginia or Chili Straw- berry, neither will the pollen of the latter two species fer- tilize the pistils of the former. But the Virginia and Chili Strawberries are so closely allied that they readily hybridize ; consequently, varieties of either may be em- ployed as the male or pollen-bearing for pistillate varie- ties, provided, of course, that they bloom at the same time, that is, the plants that are to yield the pollen and those to receive it must bloom together.

There is a great difference in the potency of the pol- len of the different varieties of plants of the same spe- cies, and it is not at all rare to find bisexual plants the pollen of which will not fertilize their own ovaries, while it is perfectly potent when applied to the stigmas of another plant of the same species. Thus one variety of the Strawberry may, in appearance, have perfect flowers, and in the greatest abundance, and both stamens and pistils be fully developed, and still ninety per cent. or even more of the flowers will fail to produce fruit. In such instances of non-productiveness we may be quite certain that there is something wrong in the sexual or-

gans, but it may be very difficult or impossible to determine what it is.

At a very extensive exhibition of Strawberries held at
the *American Agriculturist* office.N. Y., on June 18th,
19th and 20th, 1863, I was awarded, among other prizes,
the one offered for the "best flavored variety." This
was one of the many unnamed seedlings then growing
in my grounds, and, although a fine fruit in appearance
and flavor, it was utterly worthless owing to the unpro-
ductiveness of the plants, and for this reason it was never
distributed. The plants were hardy, blossomed freely,
and to all outward appearance the flowers were perfect ;
still neither their own pollen or that from other varieties
would fertilize the pistils except in rare instances.
Every one who has attempted to raise new varieties of
the Strawberry must have had a similar experience, some
being very productive and others almost barren, and yet
their sexual organs may have appeared to be perfect.
With a large majority of the bisexual or perfect flowered
varieties self-fertilization is the rule, but occasionally a
little outside aid in supplying pollen may be beneficial,
and in instances of this kind the raising of several varieties in close proximity will largely increase the yield of
fruit.

The pistils of each flower must be supplied with a
certain amount of pollen from some source, else no fruit
will be produced. If only a part of the pistils are fertilized, a deformed fruit will be the result, because the
enlarging of the receptacle is for the sole purpose of sup-
porting the seeds resting upon its surface; therefore, we
may say, no seeds, no fruit. It has been claimed by many
vegetable physiologists that the influence of the pollen
reaches no further than the seed, but upon a close in-
spection of the flower of a Strawberry we find that the

receptacle, embryo seed and all other parts are formed and in progress towards perfection before any pollen is seen, and yet, if the latter fails to do its work, or is impotent, the entire structure decays, and even the fruit stems and their appendages wither away. In conducting some of my earlier experiments with the Strawberry, I noticed that the influence of the pollen did extend beyond the seed, for it not only caused the receptacle to enlarge and reach maturity but often changed its form and flavor. This was most readily observed when employing different staminate or perfect flowered varieties for supplying pollen to the pistillates. But as in all similar experiments in the fertilization of the ovaries, the results were not uniform, showing that the female plant often exercises such a powerful influence over its own seed and seed-vessels as to effectually obscure that of the pollen-bearing or male plant. It is not to be supposed, however, that because an effect is not prominently apparent that it does not exist.

In the first edition of "The Small Fruit Culturist," 1867, I casually referred to this subject of the influence of the pollen upon the character of the fruit, for I had previously discovered that in raising the pistillate varieties, the staminate employed for supplying their flowers with pollen had more or less influence on the size and form of the fruit of the former. It is probably unnecessary to state that this has been denied by many cultivators of the Strawberry up to the present time, while others who have carefully experimented for the purpose of determining the truth, admit that the influence of the pollen does reach beyond the seed and is often readily seen in the changed form of the fruit. But as I have discussed this subject quite fully in another work,* it is

*Propagation of Plants.

only necessary to say here that in cultivating pistillate varieties of the Strawberry, it is better to select a large and good flavored one to supply it with pollen than one that is small and of inferior quality.

STRUCTURE OF THE PLANTS.

If we closely examine the varieties of any one species of the Strawberry, we find that they resemble each other in their general habits or manner of growth. No one at all familiar with these plants would ever mistake an Alpine Strawberry for one of any other of the well-known species, and even the Hautbois Strawberry, which, in some respects, resembles the Alpines, is sufficiently distinct to be easily recognized. There are varieties of the Wood or Alpine species that produce no runners, growing in clumps or stools ; still the foliage plainly shows their origin, and, as we have no hybrids between the Alpines and other species, there is no difficulty in recognizing them wherever found. But with the North and South American species or Virginian and Chilian Strawberries the line of demarcation is not so easily determined as formerly, because they hybridize so readily that their specific characteristics have become almost obliterated in the cultivated varieties.

The Chili Strawberry in its wild state produces larger and milder flavored fruit than our common American or Virginia Strawberry, and probably for this reason it has been a favorite with the cultivators of the Strawberry in Europe, and nearly all of the noted varieties raised abroad are of this species. This is why so few of the European varieties, as they are termed, succeed in this country, having descended from a semi-tropical species. But in recent years the European and native sorts have been crossed and so thoroughly intermingled that it is

Fig. 6.—VIRGINIA STRAWBERRY.

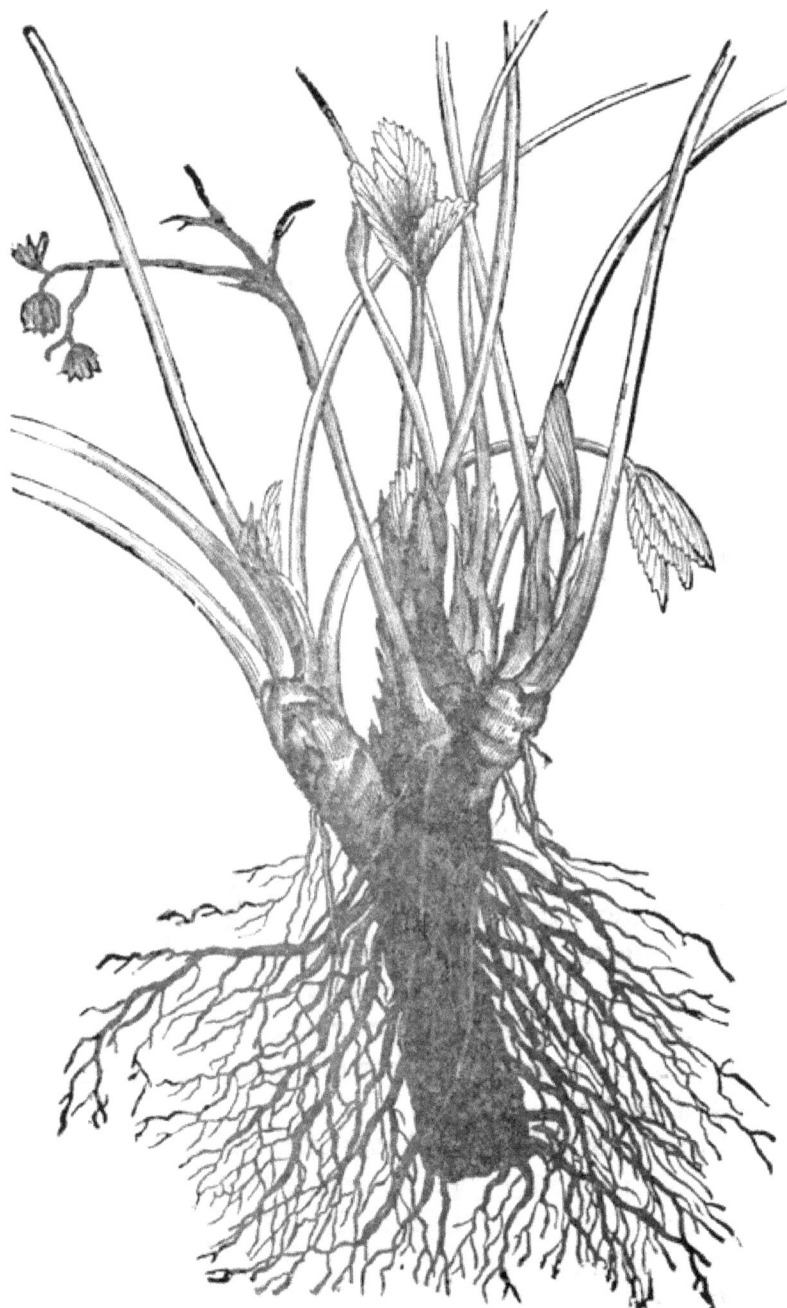

Fig. 7.—CHILI STRAWBERRY.

only occasionally that we can detect the peculiar and distinct characteristics of either species in the common cultivated varieties.

In the old Triomphe de Gand Strawberry we have a
pure descendant of the Chilian species, and in the Wilson's Albany and Charles Downing, pure native blood.
The Wilson may be considered as a large representative of
the Wild Strawberry of the Eastern States, and the Downing of the Western or of *F. Virginiana* var. *Illinoensis.*

The varieties of our native species usually have long
thread-like or wiry roots, which penetrate the soil deeply
and spread widely in search of nutriment and moisture,
while the roots of the pure Chilian varieties appear to be
more fleshy, shorter and not so hard and firm.

Another peculiarity in the form and structure may
be observed by an examination of the old and mature
plants. In our native varieties, like the Downing and
Boston Pine, they appear to remain low down in the soil
—not inclined to push above the surface—dividing naturally, as shown in Fig. 6, while the Chilian varieties assume the form shown in Fig. 7, which is an exact represen-
tation—half natural size—of a three year old plant of the
Triomphe de Gand. It will be observed, by examining
the illustration, that all of the crowns are united to the
main or central one, with little inclination to separate
from it. These elevated crowns contain the embryo
fruit-buds, and the more they extend above the surface
of the soil the more likely they are to be injured by the
frosts of winter.

Varieties of this form of root or crown soon extend so
far above the surface that their new roots cannot, or at
least do not, take a firm hold of the soil in sufficient numbers to supply the plant with nutriment.

There are many excellent varieties in cultivation that

are inclined to assume this form of growth, and they require somewhat different treatment from those with shorter and low-spreading crowns, as shown in Fig. 6. When the latter are cultivated in hills or single rows, the soil may be drawn up against the plants as their crowns protrude above the surface, covering the new lateral roots, thereby increasing the vigor and prolonging the life of the plants.

PROPAGATION.

The three most common modes of propagation of the Strawberry are, viz., by seeds, runners and divisions of the crowns or stools. The first mode, or by seeds, is practiced mostly for the purpose of producing new varieties, but the wild plants of all the species reproduce themselves from seed with very slight variations, and it is only from the already improved varieties that we can expect to raise new ones of any considerable value. If, however, we fertilize the pistils of a wild plant with pollen from an improved one, we stand a fair chance of obtaining seedlings showing an advance upon the wild or parent plant. However, unless there is some special object in view—such as extreme hardiness, or the adaptation of a variety to a certain soil or situation—it is better to save seed from the improved sorts than to go back or resort to the primitive or wild species for a supply.

To obtain seed it is only necessary to select the ripe berries, and either crush the pulp and spread it out and dry it with the seeds, thus preserving both, or the fruit may be crushed and the seeds washed out. The sound good seeds will fall to the bottom, and the pulp and false ones remain on the surface, from which both may be readily removed. I have found seed preserved in the dried pulp of the Strawberry remain sound and good for several years, and, if it is to be kept for any considerable time, I should much prefer to have it preserved in the pulp than to have it removed or washed out, but the berries should be thoroughly dried and then put away in paper bags as usually practised with clean seeds. I have received dried Strawberries from Europe that were several years old, the seeds of which, when soaked and washed out, sprouted almost as readily as fresh ones.

My usual practice in raising seedling Strawberries has been to gather the largest and best berries, then mix them with dry sand, crushing the pulp between the hands and so thoroughly manipulating the mass that no two seeds will remain together. Then set away the box containing the sand and seed in some cool place until the following spring. Then sow the sand and seed together either in some half-shady situation in the garden, or in pots, boxes or frames. The soil in which the seed is sown should be of a light texture, to prevent baking of the surface after watering. The seed should be scattered on the surface, and fine soil sifted over them to a depth of not more than one-quarter of an inch, or less than one-eighth. Apply water freely with a watering pot or garden syringe, using a fine rose in order that the water shall fall on the surface in the form of spray instead of a stream, as the latter is likely to wash out the seed. By keeping the soil moist the plants will usually appear in two to four weeks after sowing, and, if sown under glass or in warm weather, in less time.

If the plants do not come up so thickly as to be crowded, they may remain in the seedbed during the entire season, but usually it is better to transplant them into rows in the open ground where they can have more room for development. All runners should be removed the first season in order to secure as vigorous growth of the original plant as possible. The following season the plants will bear fruit, when the best and most promising may be preserved and the others destroyed. It must not, however, be expected that a one-year-old seedling is a fully developed plant, and for this reason it is well to preserve all which give promise of excellence.

If the seed is sown as soon as it is removed from the freshly-gathered fruit in summer, it will sprout in two or three weeks, and produce plants with several well developed leaves before the end of the season, and, if given protection the first winter, they will make a vigorous growth the next, and become somewhat larger plants than those raised from seed sown in the spring of the same year. It is best to give the seedlings some protection in cold climates in order to secure their full development.

When the plants come into bloom they should be carefully examined, and those with pistillate flowers—as these will usually be the least numerous—marked so that they will be known when the fruit is ripe. When a variety has been raised that promises to be valuable, the plant should be carefully lifted during rainy weather and set out by itself for propagation.

The plants may be removed from the seedling bed or rows soon after the fruit is mature, or its character fully determined if carefully lifted, and then given plenty of water and shaded a few days after re-planting. It is not at all difficult to raise new varieties, but to obtain one worthy of propagation and dissemination is quite another matter, and the chances are not more than one in a thousand of obtaining a new variety from seed equal to the best of the old ones now in cultivation. It is well enough, however, for every person who has the

time to spare and inclination to experiment, to try, because there is not only a chance of producing varieties
better than any now in cultivation, but in addition the
pleasure of watching one's own seedlings grow and bear
fruit.

Propagation by Runners.—This is the natural
method of propagation of all the species and varieties except the Bush Alpines.   The first runner produced on a
plant in summer is usually the strongest and best for
early removal, but those that are produced later in the
season on the same runner are equally as good when of
the same age and size.   Certain theorists have, however,
claimed that the first plant formed on a runner near the
parent plant was naturally stronger and better in every
way than those following or produced later, but long experience has not proved this to be true.   If the second,
third or fourth plant should happen to thrust its roots
into richer soil than the first one, they will become the
larger and stronger plants before the end of the season.
To insure the rooting of the young plants, the surface of
the soil should be kept loose and open, and if a top
dressing of fine old manure can be applied just before or
at the time the runners are pushing out most rapidly, it
will greatly facilitate the production of roots.

Pot Plants.—In the last few years what are called
" pot-grown plants" have become very popular among
amateur cultivators, who may desire to purchase a few
plants and have them in the best possible condition to
insure rapid growth and early planting.   To accommo-
date this class of buyers our Strawberry growers have made
these pot-grown or layered plants a distinct feature of
their business.   In propagating plants by this mode
small two or three-inch flower pots are filled with rich

soil and then plunged in the ground, around the old stools and in such positions as will admit of placing a young plant while attached to the runner in each, or on the surface of the soil in the pot so that the new roots will penetrate it. When the new plants have produced a sufficient number of roots in these pots to form a somewhat compact mass or ball of the earth within, they are carefully separated, the pots lifted, and either sent to the purchasers in the pots or knocked out, and each plant rolled up separately in a piece of paper or some similar material.

Plants that have become well established in the pots in time for planting out early in the fall will often yield a moderate crop of fruit the following season, which the amateur cultivator may value far more highly than the professional who raises fruit for market. Pot-grown plants cost more than those raised in the ordinary way, and they are worth more, especially to persons who are anxious to test a new variety or see Strawberries ripening in their own garden.

PROPAGATION BY DIVISION.

This mode is seldom practiced except with the Bush Alpines, which do not produce runners. To propagate these varieties the old stools should be lifted early in Spring and divided, leaving only one or two crowns to a plant. If the old or central stems are very long, the lower or older part may be cut away, leaving only the upper and younger roots attached. In setting out again, the crown of the plant should be just level with the surface of the soil in order that new lateral roots may spring out above the old ones on the central stalk or stem.

In its wild state the Strawberry is found growing in a great variety of soils, from the rich alluvial deposits

SOIL AND ITS PREPARATION.

along rivers, up to the sand hills and even bleak rocky ridges of Alpine regions. But as the largest species and varieties are found growing in the richest soils, so in cultivation we will ever find that large fruit, and this in abundance, can only be secured by supplying a corresponding amount of nutriment. New soils, free from weeds and noxious insects, are certainly preferable to old, worn and badly infested; but as the Strawberry grower can seldom have his choice in such matters, he must use such as he has and overcome natural obstacles with artificial remedies. A rather light soil or what would be called loamy soil, is preferable to heavy clay, or the opposite extreme as seen in sand and gravel. But natural defects can usually be remedied, for the stiff cold clay can be improved by underdraining and subsoiling, also by adding vegetable matter in large quantities. The main point to be observed is to secure a good depth of soil with good drainage and plenty of nutriment for the plants. Next in importance after supplying what may be termed the substantial elements in the form of nutriment comes moisture, for the Strawberry plant will use an immense amount if it is obtainable, but stagnant water at the roots or a constantly water-soaked soil are conditions to be avoided. A soil that will allow the water falling in the form of rain to pass down through it in a few hours, and still hold enough in suspension to keep it moist for weeks, is a proper one for the Strawberry, whatever may have been its original nature or condition.

Land that will produce a good crop of corn or potatoes may be considered in a fair condition for Strawberries, provided that it is not so situated as to be in danger of flooding during the time of the usual overflow of streams in winter and spring. But the Strawberry requires a deeper soil than corn, and this may be readily secured by deep plowing, or what is better, turning over the surface soil shallow, and following with a subsoil plow, and in this way avoid bringing the poorer subsoil to the surface. The land, if naturally hard and compact, should be cross-plowed in the same way, and, if manure is to be applied at all, let it be spread over the surface before the first plowing, in order that it may become well mixed and intermingled with the soil before the plants are set out, that is, if ordinary kinds of composts or barn-yard manure are used. When commercial manures are employed they are usually applied in the form of top-dressings at the time of setting out the plants, or at various times afterwards as the plants may show the need of more stimulants and nutriment.

Manures.—The Strawberry is not so capricious as to refuse nutriment in almost any form when presented to its roots, but the quantity and quality may be varied according to circumstances. On the rich prairies of the Western States, or on newly-cleared land in the East, no manure may be necessary in order to secure a heavy crop of fruit, but the plants require nutriment in abundance, and, if it is not natural in the soil, we must place it there in some form. As for the kind of fertilizer to use, I have never, as yet, found anything to excel thoroughly decomposed barn-yard manure. On light, warm, sandy soils I prefer cow manure to that of the horse, as it is of a cooler nature, but if manure from barn yard or stables is left in the yard until it has become well rotted, or is composted with muck, leaves and similar materials, it may be used on sandy soils, and in liberal amounts without danger of over stimulating the plants. Bone dust, superphosphate of lime, sulphate of ammonia, muriate of potash, and wood ashes, may all be used where the land is poor or extra stimulants are needed to force the growth and increase the size of the fruit.

HOW AND WHEN TO PLANT.

While it is perfectly practicable to transplant the Strawberry at any and all seasons of the year—except when the ground is hard frozen and covered with snow—still there appear to be certain months during which this operation may be performed with less labor and more uniform success than during any other of the twelve. In warm climates, as in our Southern States, the best time for setting out the plants is late in the autumn or at almost any time during the winter, but the earlier the better, in order to secure the benefits of the cool moist weather during which the plants become well established and in condition for growth at the approach of warm weather in spring. But in cold climates late fall planting will, in most instances, result in a total loss, as the frosts of winter will lift the plants from the soil and destroy them. The two seasons most favorable for planting the Strawberry in cold climates are early fall, or from the middle of August to the first week in September and early in the Spring. Fall planting, however, of the Strawberry is not generally practiced in the Northern States except by amateurs and with pot-grown plants. But in this matter of transplanting much depends upon the season ; if there is an abundance of rain during the summer, strong, well-rooted plants may be obtained in August or by the first of September, and if these are set out, and the weather continues favorable, they will become well established by the time cold weather sets in, and the following season make a much better growth than if the planting was delayed until spring. But favorable seasons are so uncertain that autumn planting is not a general practice among those who make Strawberry culture a specialty.

When transplanting in the spring, the half-dead

Fig. 8.—YOUNG STRAWBERRY PLANT.

leaves should be removed and the roots shortened one-third or one-half their length. In Fig. 8 is shown a terminal plant on a runner as taken from the ground. A, the runner connecting it with the parent plant. B, the tip of the runner which would have extended and produced another plant had it not been checked by frost.

C—D, the cross line showing the point at which the roots should be cut. This pruning or shortening of the roots causes the production of a new set of fibres from the severed ends. It also causes other roots to push out from near the crown, and if a plant thus pruned be taken up in a few weeks after planting, its roots will appear

Fig. 9.—PLANT WITH ROOTS PRUNED.

somewhat as shown in Fig. 9. This pruning of the roots is not so generally practiced as it deserves to be, especially with plants that have been out of the ground for several days, or until the roots are withered or have

commenced to decay at the ends. No matter how carefully the plants are taken up, some of the fibres will be
broken off, and it is much better to sever all the roots
with a clean cut than to plant them with ragged and
broken ends. Roots pruned in this way are more readily
spread out when placed in the ground again than when
left intact or of full length.

Selection of Plants.—Young runners of one season's growth are best, and old plants should not be used
for transplanting, if it can be avoided. But, if a variety
is scarce and valuable, the old stools may be taken up
and pulled apart, and the lower end of the central stalk
cut away as recommended for the Bush Alpines, and
then set out again, planting deep enough to ensure the
emission of new roots above the old ones.

DIFFERENT MODES OF CULTIVATION.

The cultivators of the Strawberry are not all of one
opinion in regard to the best mode of cultivation either
in the field or garden ; consequently, we hear much
about raising Strawberries in hills, rows, matted beds,
annual renewal systems, etc., all of which may give good
results, with productive varieties and on rich soils.

But different varieties often require a different mode
of culture in order to obtain the largest yield and the
largest berries. The large, coarse-grown varieties of the
Chili species, or the hybrid between these and the Virginia Strawberry, succeed best when grown in hills or single rows, and they are usually quite unproductive if the
plants are permitted to run together and become in the
least crowded. The Triomphe de Gand, Jucunda,
Champion, Agriculturist and Lennig's White are well-
known varieties of this type ; while others, such as
Charles Downing, President Wilder, Green Prolific and

Manchester, will yield well either in narrow rows or wide beds, and where the plants become matted.

In the "hill system" the plants are usually set out in rows about three feet apart, and the plants eighteen inches to two feet apart in the row. The ground is kept thoroughly cultivated among the plants during the entire season, and all runners removed as soon as they appear, or at least once a week. This treatment will insure very large and strong plants, with numerous crowns or buds, from which fruit-stalks will push up the following spring. In cold climates and where the plants are likely to be exposed to alternate freezing and thawing, or to cold winds during the winter, they should be protected by a light covering of hay, coarse manure, or some similar material—just enough to protect the crowns from injury—but not enough to prevent freezing. In the spring the materials used for protection may be removed, and the plants given a good hoeing or a cultivator run between the rows to soften up the soil, which may have become hard and compact during the winter; but this cultivation in the spring will depend somewhat upon the character of the soil, for, if it is light and of a sandy nature, it will not be necessary, but it will certainly do no harm and may prove of great benefit to the plants. After the beds are cleared up and before the plants come into bloom, the entire surface of the ground should be covered with long straw or some similar material as a mulch to keep the soil moist and the fruit clean when it ripens. It is almost a waste of time to undertake to raise the large varieties in hills without mulching the plants, for the largest berries are almost certain to become splashed with soil during heavy rains.

When grown in single rows the plants may be set about twelve inches apart in the rows, and for garden culture the rows should be about three feet apart, but for field culture I prefer to allow a little more space between the rows, or four feet, but the distance may be varied according to the habit of the plants—some of the rank-growing varieties requiring more room than those of a medium growth, but it is much better to allow the plants plenty of room than to have them crowded.

During the first season the plants must be given good cultivation, and the more the soil is stirred among them the better, provided the roots are not disturbed by the implements employed in this work. In the field a one-horse cultivator is the best implement to use for keeping the soil loose and free from weeds between the rows, and, while the hoe may be used early in the season to stir the surface about the plants, it will have to be abandoned later on when the runners push out, for these are to be allowed to take root in the row, and form a bed about one foot wide, and all that extend out beyond this may be cut off or torn up with the cultivator. Some cultivators allow the runners to take root over a space of eighteen to twenty-four inches wide, leaving just room enough between the narrow beds to give a path in which to stand in gathering the fruit the following season. It is doubtful, however, if any more fruit will be obtained from a larger number of small plants than from less but of a stronger and more vigorous growth, as they are more likely to be, if restricted to a narrow row.

If protection in winter is necessary—and usually it is in our Northern States—it should be given as soon as the ground begins to freeze in the fall or early winter. If applied before the weather has become cool and the nights frosty, there is danger of the plants sweating and bleaching. Still, it is not well to delay covering up until snow falls and prevents it.

Coarse, strong manure from the **stable or barnyard,** scattered along over the crowns of the plants, makes an excellent winter protection, but as such material contains many weed seeds, it should be employed only on beds that are to be plowed up after fruiting the ensuing season.   **In fact,** it will seldom pay the cultivator to clean out an old weedy plantation, for it costs less to set out a new one.

Bed or Matted System.—In this mode two or three rows are planted in beds four feet wide, and the plants allowed to cover the entire surface until they form a close mat or bed ; hence the name.   One or two crops are taken and then the plants are plowed up as usual when cultivated in rows.   But, by thinning out occasionally, the beds may be kept in a moderately productive condition for several years, especially with some of the more slender growing of our native varieties.   Some cultivators, who raise Strawberries for market, adopt what may be called an annual system, setting out plants in spring either in single rows or narrow beds, giving them extra care during the first season, then, after the fruit is gathered the next summer, the beds are plowed up.   This mode necessitates the making of a new plantation annually.   On very rich soils and with the larger varieties—which generally command the highest price in market—this system is no doubt an excellent and profitable one.   But amateurs and others, who have only a limited space to devote to this fruit, will prefer either the hill or row system, because, by devoting a little more labor to cultivation and removing the runners, the beds may be kept in good condition for fruiting a half dozen years.   By an occasional top-dressing of old and well rotted manure, and forking in the materials used for protecting the plants and a mulch, the soil will be kept in fine condition for insuring a vigorous growth of plants. Old beds, however, are usually more likely to be infested by noxious insects than new ones, in addition to weeds, such as white clover, which are difficult to eradicate without disturbing the roots of the plants.

Planting.—The surface of the bed or field to be planted should be made smooth, level and free from lumps and stones. If it is uneven and there are many little hillocks and depressions, as are naturally left after plowing, the plants will follow these undulating lines, and some will be buried too deep and others have their roots exposed after the first heavy shower.

Always choose a cloudy day for planting, and it is far better to heel the plants in for a few days and give them a little water and shade than to set them out in dry weather. Draw a line where you are to set a row of plants, keeping it a few inches above the ground, so that you may plant under it instead of along one side. Use a transplanting trowel for making holes for the reception of the roots, and these should be spread out evenly in all directions, or spread apart, so that they will lie against one side of the hole made with the trowel. Cover the plants as deep as possible without covering the crowns, and then press the soil down firmly around the roots. Some cultivators use a small wooden dibber for planting, merely making a round hole in the soil into which the roots are thrust all in a clump. Plants may live under such treatment, but careful planting with a trowel is far the best mode. If the weather should prove dry after planting, watering will, of course, be beneficial ; but is only practicable on a small scale, as in gardens, or where it may be necessary to save some new and choice variety. '

Where pistillate varieties are raised for the main crop then every fourth or fifth row should be planted with some hermaphrodite or perfect flowering variety, which blooms at or about the same time as the pistillate.

If the plants are cultivated in wide beds, then about every third one should be planted with some perfect flowering sort to supply pollen to the pistillate plants. But, as I have said elsewhere, there is no need of, or good reason for, cultivating these imperfect flowering varieties at all, and, unless one should appear better than any as yet known, they might all be discarded without loss to either cultivators or consumers of this fruit.

To Raise Extra Large Fruit.—First of all secure plants of varieties known to grow to a large size, then plant in rich soil, remove the runners as soon as they appear, keep the weeds down, stir the surface of the soil frequently, apply water as often as necessary, which will be at least twice a week in dry weather, also give liquid manure occasionally; in fact, force the plants to make a strong and vigorous growth. In the fall, or at the approach of cold weather, cover the plants with hay, straw, or some similar material, and in the spring remove it and spade or fork up the ground between the rows, after which spread over the ground sufficient mulch to keep the soil moist even during the time of drought. Under such treatment extra large berries may usually be produced. The cost of raising fruit by such modes of cultivation is, of course, seldom taken into consideration, and it really ought not to be any more than any other amusement devised for our own pleasure or that of our friends.

Of course, it is not to be supposed that large and fine fruit cannot be raised without extra and expensive modes of cultivation, but I have yet to learn of an instance where "astonishing" large Strawberries have been produced without a corresponding outlay in manure, labor and care.

POT CULTURE AND FORCING.

It often occurs that Strawberries ripening out of season are far more valuable than those maturing in the usual or natural season. Ripe Strawberries in mid-winter or even a month or two in advance of the crop ripening out of doors, always command an extra price in our markets ; and, if a person does not care to raise fruit to sell, he may take pride in having them on his own table out of the regular season.

It is not at all difficult to raise Strawberry plants in pots and force them into fruiting at almost any season as desired, provided a person has a greenhouse, pit or hot-house in which the plants may be stored and forced with artificial heat during cold weather.

The plants to be forced may be of either one or two seasons' growth. If strong plants are desired and such as will produce a number of fruit-stalks, small young plants should be potted in the spring, using four or five inch pots for this purpose. The pots containing the plants should be plunged in the open ground, and where water can be given as required, and all runners removed as soon as they appear, also flower and fruit stalks. In June or July shift the plants into eight-inch pots, using very rich and compact soil. A few pieces of broken pots or old sods should be placed in the bottom of the pots for drainage, but the ball of earth about the roots must not be broken when transferring from the smaller to the larger pots. Give water to settle the soil in the pots, then plunge the pots in a frame where they will continue to grow without check until the approach of cold weather.

Plants wanted for an early crop may be brought into the house in November, as it will take from ten to twelve weeks from the time they are placed in the house before ripe fruit can be obtained. The pots may be plunged in tan or some similar material in the forcing house or merely placed on the benches or shelves, but more care is required in giving water, if the pots are exposed, than when plunged in tan or soil.

If a succession of crops is desired, then only a portion of the plants should be brought in at one time.

The temperature of the house should be only moderate at first, but increased gradually as the plants commence to grow and the fruit stems appear, when it should range from 65 to 75 degrees during the day and about ten degrees lower at night.

The plants will be benefited if syringed or watered overhead once or twice a week until they come into bloom; then omit it until the fruit is set, after which it may be continued as before. While the plants are in bloom, admit as much air as possible without lowering the temperature to a dangerous degree, and, as there will be neither wind or insects to scatter the pollen, it is usually necessary to scatter it artificially. This can be done very rapidly with an ordinary camel's hair brush or pencil, lightly touching the stamens and pistils as each flower becomes fully expanded. This is not necessary with every variety, but a larger and more uniform crop will usually be secured if practised on those fruiting most freely in the house.

The plants that are kept for forcing later in the season should be stored in a cold frame or pit, where they will remain in a dormant state until ready for use.

Plants of one season's growth or those struck in pots during the summer will answer well for forcing in winter. The plants will not be as large as older ones, or produce as many berries, but, as they are smaller, a greater number can can be forced in a given space. The first or earliest runners should be selected for this purpose, and a three or four-inch pot plunged in the ground underneath, or if roots have formed on the young plant when the pots are set in place, they may be thrust into the pot and good soil filled in about them. These pot-grown plants should be lifted early, or about the first of October, and shifted in to five or six-inch pots, filled with very rich compost and plenty of drainage—thenceforward treated as advised for older stock.

Such pot-grown plants may be fruited in the windows of an ordinary dwelling, provided the temperature does not fall below 40 or 45 degrees at night. The best varieties of the Strawberry for the purpose, however, are the Monthly Alpines, as they will thrive in a lower temperature than those of other species, and, with ordinary care, will continue to bloom and bear fruit all the year round. Fruit is not produced in any great abundance at any one season, but, the crop being a continuous one, it amounts to a pretty fair quantity during the year. As an ornamental window or greenhouse plant there are very few bearing edible fruit worthy of more care or attention than the Monthly Alpine Strawberry.

VARIETIES FOR FORCING.

Nearly all of the perfect flowering varieties succeed when forced under glass, but the largest and most prolific are to be preferred, because size and quantity are properties sought more than high flavors in a Strawberry "out of season." An eminent English authority (G.

W. Johnson) in referring to that subject in a work published some forty years ago, very truly says that " no
plant is more certain of producing a good crop, when
forced, than is the Strawberry, if properly treated ; and
none will more assuredly disappoint the gardener's hope,
after a fair promise, if he adopts the too common error
of forcing too fast." The Strawberry naturally blooms
in the spring when the nights are cool and the day temperature far lower than later in the season ; consequently,
a high temperature is neither required nor beneficial to
plants when first placed in the forcing house. Air
should be admitted freely during the night, and the temperature kept low until the plants come into bloom, then
an increase of several degrees is admissible, but at no
time is a very high temperature required.

The larger varieties, such as Sharpless, Miner's Prolific, Seth Boyden, Cumberland Triumph, and American
Agriculturist, are all excellent sorts for forcing, especially when extra size berries are an object.

In Europe forcing the Strawberry is practised more
extensively than in this country, but the demand for
this fruit out of its natural season is constantly increasing, and will, no doubt, continue to increase for many
years to come. Twenty-five years ago the Strawberry
season in our large cities scarcely extended beyond a
period of six weeks, but now it is nearly six months, for
ripe Strawberries come North from the Gulf States before
the frost has left the ground in the Northern, and before
these two early berries reach us from the South, those
raised by forcing houses may be found in limited quantities in our fruit stores. Of course, this early or forced
fruit commands a high price, but those who are able and
willing to pay for such luxuries should be, and are
usually, accommodated.

FORCING HOUSES.

Almost any ordinary greenhouse may be used as a forcing house for the Strawberry, provided it is so constructed that the plants can be placed near the glass. If the plants are placed several feet below the roof or glass, they are likely to be drawn, as it is termed, the leaves and fruit-stalks growing tall and slender. Low houses are, therefore, better for this purpose than high ones, and even low-walled pits, heated by brick flues or earthern pipes, answer well for forcing the Strawberry.

INSECT ENEMIES.

Until within the past decade or two the Strawberry was rarely injured—at least not to any extent—by either insect or disease. But as its cultivation is extended it naturally encounters a greater number of enemies. Probably the most destructive pest is known under the common name of White Grub, or larva of the May Beetle. There are, however, over sixty distinct species of the May Beetle inhabiting the United States, but, as their habits are very nearly the same, they may for all practical purposes be considered as one. There is scarcely a mile square of good arable land in the United States that will not yield to the careful collector at least a half dozen species of *Lachnosterna* or May Beetles. They are more or less abundant in the Gulf States, and northward to Canada; thence westward to California and along the entire Pacific coast. These insects are usually more abundant in grass-lands, prairies, meadows and pastures than elsewhere, as the principal food of the grubs is the roots of grass and small herbs like the Strawberry. They sometimes become so abundant in meadows and pastures that, if such land is plowed up and planted with Strawberries, the grub will destroy every plant almost as soon as it is put into the ground. As these insects remain in the grub stage two or three years, they consume a large amount of food, and they appear to prefer the roots of the Strawberry to those of the common kinds of grasses.

Owing to the wide distribution of these insects, and their almost universal presence in old meadows and pastures, these lands should be avoided whenever possible. If broken up and cultivated for a year or two, or until the grubs have passed into the beetle stage, there can be no objection to such lands if otherwise adapted to the Strawberry. The female beetles usually resort to uncultivated fields to deposit their eggs; consequently they are not likely to become very abundant in those that are constantly kept under cultivation.

The Strawberry worm (*Emphytus maculatus*) is occasionally very abundant and destructive. It is a small, slender, pale-green worm about five-eighths of an inch long, attacking the leaves, eating large holes in them at first, but eventually entirely denuding the plant of foliage. Dusting the plants with lime when the leaves are wet with dew, or with Paris green, will usually check this pest.

In Canada and some of the Western States an insect known as the Strawberry Leaf-Roller is occasionally quite abundant and destructive. It is the larva or caterpiller of a small and handsome moth, the *Anchylopera fragaria*. It is quite probable that Paris green would be an effective remedy and might be safely used after the fruit was gathered in summer.

There are also several species of beetles that attack the crowns and stalks of the Strawberry, and the common Strawberry Crown-borer (*Tyloderma fragaria*) attacks the embryo fruit-stalks in the spring, thereby destroying the most important organ of the plants. The only remedy known is to immediately plow under the plants and destroy the grubs while in an immature stage. In my own experience, however, I have never, as yet, encountered an insect enemy of the Strawberry which could not be readily vanquished by clean cultivation and frequent renewal of the beds on plantation.

VARIETIES.

What varieties to plant is one of the puzzling questions which every inexperienced cultivator desires to have answered. If he consults the catalogues of dealers, he is certain to find that the newest and highest-priced variety is the one above all others that he should select. But if he pursues his investigations a little farther in this direction, and examines the lists of a dozen different dealers in plants, he will probably find that no two agree, each having some special variety to offer, as the very best and most promising one known. But as society is now constituted it is considered as perfectly legitimate for a dealer to extol his wares, even far above what their merit would warrant if the actual truth about them was told ; consequently, we are not surprised to be informed by the introducer of new varieties, that each and every one offered is far superior to anything of the kind heretofore known. " Yielding double the quantity of any other variety" has become a stereotyped phrase in advertising new varieties, and yet every experienced cultivator of Strawberries knows that the Wilson, introduced nearly thirty years ago, has never been excelled in productiveness. A variety, which, under the same conditions, would produce double the quantity of this old **favorite,** might certainly be considered something unique in the way of a Strawberry.

Strange as it may appear to the novice in fruit culture, varieties which are most highly praised at their introduction, are quite frequently the first to disappear from cultivation, while others gain a prominent position in spite of all opposition. The Wilson, when first exhibited, and for years afterwards, met with opposition and was denounced as unfit for cultivation or use by some of the most prominent pomologists in the country. Yet it continued to grow in favor until, within the past decade or less, it was more extensively cultivated than any other variety, and probably there were more acres planted with it than all the others put together, and even at this late day it is considered a standard and profitable berry.

This variety was said to be too acid and too dark colored for a market berry, and the late berries on the plant were too small, all of which is true, but the fruit is very firm, withstands long carriage and rough handling, and when it comes to filling the baskets and crates at gathering time the Wilson rarely disappointed the cultivator or consumer, who sought the markets for his supply of Strawberries.

The lesson to be learned from the erratic reputation of the Wilson is that first impressions are not always trustworthy, and a variety may prove better than it promises when first introduced, although it must be admitted that the chances are ten to one against the very best of new sorts.

In the following select list of varieties I propose mentioning only those which have gained a local or widespread reputation for excellence, without regard to the length of time they may have been in cultivation. Pistillate varieties are indicated by the letter P.

Agriculturist.—Very large, irregular, conical; with long neck, large specimens often flattened or coxcomb shape; color light red or reddish crimson. A large and valuable variety for garden culture, but when cultivated in beds the fruit is only of medium size, as shown in Fig. 10.

Bidwell.—Large, irregular, conical; bright scarlet; flesh only moderately firm; quality excellent. A vigorous grower, and in heavy soils quite productive. Its reputation as a market variety is rather local.

Black Defiance.—Large, irregular in shape; dark glossy crimson; flesh moderately firm; high flavored. Color too dark and dull for market, but a good berry for home use.

Brooklyn Scarlet.—Medium to large, regular conical with neck, as shown in Fig. 11; color bright light scarlet; flesh rather soft, sweet and rich; quality best. An excellent variety for home use, but now rarely seen in cultivation.

Fig. 10.—AMERICAN AGRICULTURIST.

Champion (*Windsor Chief.—P.*)—Large round; bright crimson; flesh rather soft and of a spicy acid flavor, only second best. Plants vigorous and exceedingly productive when planted in rich soils and near a variety yielding an abundance of pollen.

Charles Downing.—Medium to large, round obtuse conical; very regular in form; bright scarlet, becoming darker when fully ripe; flesh moderately firm, pink, juicy, with a rich, sprightly subacid flavor.   One of the very best and most popular varieties in cultivation, and now extensively cultivated for market in all

of our Northern States.   The plants are very hardy and yield a heavy crop when cultivated in rows or matted beds.

Crescent.—Medium to large, somewhat irregular conical ; bright scarlet ; flesh rather soft for a market berry, but will carry well for a short distance ; quality fair but not rich ; the plants, however, are so productive that this variety has been called "The lazy man's berry."

Fig. 11.—BROOKLYN
SCARLET.

Cumberland Triumph (*Jumbo*).—Very large obtuse conical, but under high culture, or when forced under glass, is somewhat irregular ; light bright scarlet ; flesh pale pink of excellent flavor.   A vigorous grower and very productive in strong fertile soils.   Very popular among amateur cultivators of the Strawberry.

Downer's Prolific.—Medium, globular, light scarlet ; seed deeply imbedded ; flesh rather soft, acid, not rich, but highly perfumed.   This is an old variety, but so very hardy and prolific that it is still cultivated more or less extensively for market.

Durand.—Large, oblong or oblong conical (Fig. 12), sometimes flattened, seeds but slightly imbedded ;

color scarlet; flesh firm, solid; nearly white, of good flavor. This variety has only a moderate local reputation among amateurs.

Forest Rose.—Large, ir-regular, obtuse conical; bright scarlet; flesh firm, of good flavor.; a superior market variety, but does not succeed well in all kinds of soils that are usually considered well adapted to the Strawberry. (Fig. 13).

Glendale.—Large, regular, conical; dull scarlet; flesh firm, acid, not first quality, but a valuable late variety for market. Succeeds best on rather firm soils and poorly on sandy land.

Fig. 12.—DURAND.

Green Prolific.—Large round; pale crimson or deep scarlet; seeds slightly sunken, rather soft, acid, without richness, but highly perfumed. A wonderfully hardy and productive variety; extensively cultivated a few years since for market, as it succeeds on a great variety of soils, and when left to grow with little or no cultivation. Fig. 14 shows a berry about average size from matted rows and beds.

Fig. 13.—FOREST ROSE.

Hovey (*P.*).—Large conical; bright crimson; sub-

2

acid, sprightly and good. The oldest American variety of any note, and, although it has been in constant cultivation for nearly a half century, it is still popular in restricted localities, and especially in Massachusetts where it originated. Three prizes are offered for the Hovey by the "Massachusetts Horticultural Society" at its forthcoming Strawberry Exhibition, June 21 and 22.

Fig. 14.—GREEN PRO-LIFIC.

Jewell.—Very large, obtuse conical; bright crimson; very firm and of fine flavor. This variety was awarded a silver medal by the Massachusetts Horticultural Society in 1880. Highly recommended for home use and market.

Jessie.—This new variety was raised in 1880 by Mr. F. W. Loudon, of Wisconsin; it is a seedling of the Sharpless, and partakes of all the most desirable qualities of its parent. The originator describes the plant as "a stout, luxuriant grower, with light-green, large and clean foliage, which has never shown signs of rust; the berry very large, continuing of good size to the last picking; it is of beautiful red color, fine quality, good form, colors even with no white tips, and is firm enough for shipping great distances." From all that I can learn about this new variety it seems to be well worthy of trial

Jucunda.—Large conical; bright crimson, excellent flower; a strong and vigorous grower on rich and heavy soils, but almost worthless on light or sandy soils. A foreign variety, first disseminated in this country under the name of Knox's 700. It is still cultivated about Boston but rarely elsewhere. (Fig. 15).

Kentucky.—Medium to large, conical; bright scarlet; flesh white, moderately firm, excellent flavor; ripens late and continues in fruit a long time. Plants vigorous, hardy and very productive. Succeeds well on light soils.

Lennig's White.—Large obtuse conical; seed prominent and of a pink or light crimson color in the sun; fruit almost white, but with a delicate blush on the side exposed to the sun.

Fig. 15.—JUCUNDA.

This is evidently a seedling of the Chili species, and it is rather tender and unproductive, but withal an excellent variety.

Miner's Great Prolific.—Large to very large; somewhat irregular but inclining to a globular form; deep bright crimson; flesh pink, firm and of good flavor; plant vigorous, leaves large, light green, quite glossy. A very popular variety among amateurs as well as those who cultivate Strawberries extensively for market

President Wilder.—Medium, obtuse conical, very regular; seeds yellow; skin bright glossy scarlet; flesh firm, but juicy and very high flavored. One of the handsomest varieties in cultivation, but the plants are rather delicate and the leaves burn during the hot weather in summer. Said to succeed well in the New

England States, but I have not learned of its success elsewhere.

Seth Boyden.—Very large, irregular, conical with long neck ; dull crimson ; flesh firm, rather dry, sweet and of excellent flavor ; plant, extra vigorous and productive when cultivated in hills and in a rich soil.   One of the very best and most valuable of all the extra large varieties.

Sharpless.—This is another of the mammoth varieties and the more remarkable because it has proved to be all that was claimed for it when first introduced. Uniformly large ; often broadly wedge-form and wider at the top than at the calyx ; light glossy red ; flesh firm, juicy, rich and highly perfumed ; plant vigorous and productive.   One of the very best.

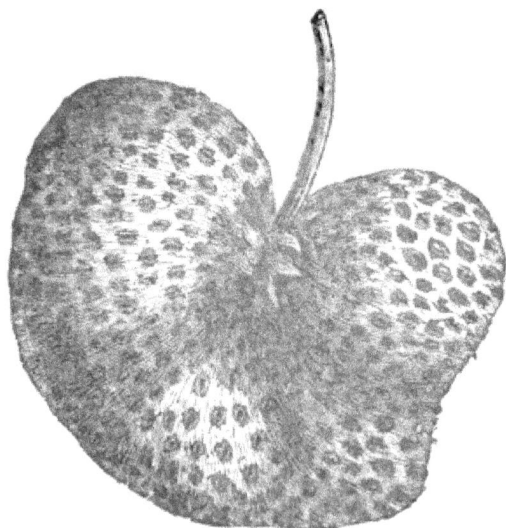

Fig. 16.—TRIOMPHE DE GAND.

Triomphe de Gand.—One of the most popular and valuable varieties ever introduced. Very large irregular, conical, but often flattened or coxcomb shape as in Fig. 16, pale or bright ; flesh very firm, crop not rich, but of a mild and pleasant flavor. This variety has probably been more extensively cultivated, and given better satisfaction than any foreign variety, and it has no superior to this day for size or production of the plants.

Wilson or Wilson's Albany.—An old and well-known variety. Large, irregular, conical; dark crimson when fully ripe ; flesh crimson, very firm, acid, but good and bears transportation well. One of the most productive varieties known.

NEWER AND LESS KNOWN VARIETIES.

Henderson.—Said to be of the largest size, early and unusually productive, and of exquisite flavor.

Indiana.—Claimed to be an improvement on the Charles Downing, but similar in size, color and quality.

Lida (*P*).—One of Mr. Durand's seedlings, claimed to be of very large size ; heart shaped ; bright red color, excellent flavor, and the plants very productive.

May King.—Seedlings of the Crescent, and resembles its parent, but the flowers are perfect. Berries are not large but ripen early and are produced in great abundance.

Old Iron Clad or Phelps.—I obtained this variety under the last name, and have been much pleased with it. Fruit medium, conical; bright crimson ; firm and rather acid but good. Plants very productive.

Parry.—Highly recommended for its large size, and has been awarded several prizes at various Strawberry shows in New York and elsewhere. Plants said to withstand droughts better than any other variety.

THE HAUTBOIS AND ALPINE STRAWBERRIES.

All of the varieties of the Hautbois Strawberry (*Fragaria elatior*) have a rather strong musky odor, which is rather disagreeable to most persons, and the fruit is usually of a dull red or greenish color and not very attractive in appearance. They are altogether inferior to the varieties of other species, and for this reason are rarely cultivated except in the gardens of botanists.

The Alpine Strawberry (*F. vesca*), on the contrary, is of a very mild flavor with a delicious perfume. There are quite a large number of varieties in cultivation in Europe, and, while none yield very large berries, they are mostly quite prolific and will thrive in cold exposed positions where those of other species would perish.

In the catalogues of European nurserymen and those who make Strawberry growing a specialty, we may find thirty or more varieties of the Alpine Strawberry described, but the larger proportion of the names used in these catalogues are mere synonyms, and it would probably be difficult to find a dozen really distinct varieties of this species in all Europe. There are, however, four really distinct varieties, all long known in this country, and now generally cultivated in European countries although under various names. These are :

Red-Bush Alpine.—Fruit medium size, conical, bright red ; seeds prominent, not sunken as usual in the common Strawberry ; flavor mild, not highly but delicately perfumed. Plants continue bearing from June till checked by frosts in autumn. In rich soils the plants will yield well throughout the entire season. As they produce no runners they must be propagated by divisions.

White-Bush Alpine.—In every respect the same as last except the fruit is pure white.

Red-Monthly Alpine.—Fruit very similar but usually a little larger than that of the Bush-Alpines, but plants produce runners freely, and the new plants on the runners bloom and bear fruit the first season, thereby keeping up a succession of berries from June to the close of the season.

White-Monthly Alpine.—This is a variety of the last, but with pure white fruit. The Monthly Alpines with runners are elegant conservatory plants, or they may be used for trailing over wire screens and for hanging baskets in window gardening.

Profits of Strawberry Culture.

Persons who have had no experience in raising Strawberries, but are considering the subject of cultivating them for market, are usually very desirous of ascertaining in advance what the prospects are for deriving a profit on their proposed investment. Unfortunately, however, for the would-be investor in such an enterprise, results depend greatly upon circumstances, such as available markets within a reasonable distance ; plenty of labor at a moderate price and at a season when needed most ; cheap lands and fertilizers, and last, but not least, favorable seasons. If a man must depend upon hired labor to gather his fruit he is never certain, in these days of "Strikes," what it is going to cost him to gather and prepare it for market. The most clear profit made in the cultivation of the Strawberry for market is by the small farmers and gardeners in the suburbs or within a moderate distance of our large cities, who have

children to assist in gathering the fruit or can always
depend upon those of their neighbors to lend a hand
when needed.   An acre of Strawberries under high cultivation, with the fruit gathered and marketed in the
very best condition, will often yield more clear profit to
the grower than ten acres under opposite conditions.

Circumstances have changed since the first edition
of this little treatise was written, for at that time our
large cities and villages were wholly supplied with small
fruit, by the farmers and gardeners in their immediate
vicinity, and, if the seasons were unfavorable, the price
of fruit advanced in proportion, and the grower was sure
of obtaining a fair remuneration for his labor whether
he had a large or limited crop of fruit.   But all this is
now changed, for railroads have practically annihilated
distance in the transportation of perishable commodities
of all kinds, and the Strawberry growers of no one local-
ity or region of the country are masters of their own
local markets, for those residing a hundred or even five-
hundred miles away may become their most persistent
and successful competitors.   If a market is not fully
supplied, and prices go up in consequence, the telegraph
conveys the information to those who may be able to
supply the deficiency; hence local monopolies are no lon-
ger possible.   The Strawberry season in our Northern
cities opens with fruit from Florida, and continues until
the last crate comes in from Maine or Canada, and yet,
fresh, choice, large fruit usually commands a fairly re-
munerative price in all of our large cities and villages
throughout the entire country.

While the profits of Strawberry culture are not so
large as they were twenty or thirty years ago, still, they
are sufficient to induce those who have longest made the
cultivation of this berry a specialty, to continue in the

business. On good land, with the best and most productive varieties, one to three hundred dollars per acre
profit are usually realized, which is a far greater sum
than is generally obtained from any of the leading farm
crops.

INDEX.

www.ingramcontent.com/pod-product-compliance
Lightning Source LLC
Chambersburg PA
CBHW031754090426
42739CB00008B/1010